HOMEMADE
Dog Food
COOKBOOK for
Small Dogs

A Comprehensive Guide and Meal Plan for a Healthier Dog Life

PRELIMINARY NOTE

This cookbook isn't just about recipes; it's about the love and care we pour into every meal for our furry friends. Picture this: the sound of pots and pans clinking together, the aroma of fresh ingredients filling the air, and the anticipation in your dog's eyes as they eagerly await their next homemade delicacy. That's the lovely step you are about to take.

I can attest to the satisfaction I get from watching my dog's tail wag in excitement when I serve them something that I made with my own two hands. There's something very special about knowing exactly what goes into their bowl—no hidden ingredients, just good, healthy food.

So, if you're ready to roll up your sleeves and dive into the world of homemade dog food, grab your apron and let's get cooking! Together, we'll whip up meals that not only nourish our furry companions but also deepen the bond we share with them.

THANKS FOR GETTING THIS GREAT BOOK

Kindly leave a review on Amazon. This will mean a lot to me

Introduction: Why Homemade Dog Food?

This is my first-hand experience with dog nutrition because I am the proud owner of a lively and loving cocker spaniel named Sora. Sora entered my life as a playful pup, full of energy and joy, but as he grew older, he started to develop health issues that made me feel worried and helpless. After my 12-year-old Cocker Spaniel's diagnosis of a large mass large enough to disrupt her organs during a visit to the vet, I began cooking primarily for him to give him the best quality of life he had left. After six months, an X-ray revealed the mass had shrunk, nine months later the organs were back where they should have been, and a year later, there were no longer any scary shadows. I still cook for my dogs, and I'm very, very happy to do so. He's now 14 years old, and her body is strangely healthy due to her good diet.

Safety Considerations Before You Go Fully Homemade

In order to guarantee that your dog receives balanced nutrition without jeopardizing their health, it is imperative that safety be given top priority when making homemade dog food. The following are some critical safety considerations for anyone looking to start making homemade dog food:

- ☐ Spend some time learning about the essential nutrients dogs require to stay healthy, such as protein, carbs, fats, vitamins, and minerals.

You should also be aware of the various sources of these nutrients and how they affect your dog's general well-being.

☐ Aim for a balanced diet when making homemade dog food, which includes giving your dog the proper amounts of proteins, carbs, fats, vitamins, and minerals. You can use reliable resources, like canine nutrition books or veterinary nutritionists, to help you create balanced recipes.

☐ To minimize exposure to pesticides and other harmful substances, use organic ingredients in your homemade dog food recipes. When choosing ingredients, go for fresh, whole foods whenever possible. Ingredients that are toxic to dogs include onions, garlic, grapes, raisins, chocolate, and xylitol.

☐ When making homemade dog food, follow these guidelines for food safety and hygiene: wash your hands well before and after handling ingredients; make sure all utensils, cutting boards, and surfaces are clean and sanitized; and store ingredients correctly to avoid contamination and spoiling.

☐ Cooked bones should never be given to your dog because they can splinter and lead to choking, intestinal blockages, or damage to the mouth or digestive tract. Other foods to watch out for include avocados, macadamia nuts, alcohol, and caffeine.

☐ Control portion sizes to avoid feeding your dog too much or too little. Keep a regular eye on your dog's weight and body condition and make necessary adjustments to their food intake to keep them at a healthy weight. Refrain from giving your dog too many treats and table scraps as these can lead to nutritional imbalances and obesity.

☐ To help your dog's digestive system adjust, gradually increase the amount of homemade food your dog is fed over time by starting small and working your way up to a larger portion.

Throughout this transition period, keep an eye out for any signs of upset stomach or negative reactions in your dog.

☐ Plan routine veterinary examinations to keep an eye on your dog's health and make sure that their homemade diet is working for them. Your veterinarian can evaluate your dog's general health, offer nutritional advice, and adjust their diet plan as needed.

Essential Nutrients for Small Dogs

Even though small dog breeds are small in stature, they have nutritional needs that are just as great as those of larger dogs. Supporting small dogs' general health, energy levels, and lifespan requires optimal nutrition; knowing which essential nutrients are necessary for small dogs and how to include them in their diet is essential when changing to homemade food for your dog. The following is a detailed guide to the essential nutrients small dogs need:

- ☐ Protein: Small dogs need a higher proportion of protein in their diet than larger breeds in order to support their fast metabolism and energy levels. Choose high-quality animal-based protein sources such as lean meats (chicken, turkey, beef), fish, eggs, and dairy products.
- ☐ Fat: Feed your dog healthy fats from sources such as fish oil, flaxseed oil, chicken fat, and coconut oil into their diet to support overall health and well-being. Fat is a concentrated source of energy and plays a vital role in providing essential fatty acids, which are necessary for healthy skin, coat, and brain function.
- ☐ Carbohydrates: Choosing complex carbohydrates like whole grains

(brown rice, oats, barley), vegetables (sweet potatoes, peas, carrots), and legumes (lentils, chickpeas) will give small dogs sustained energy and fiber. Carbohydrates also support digestive health and provide essential nutrients.

☐ Vitamins: Make sure your small dog's diet consists of a balanced mix of fruits, vegetables, and fortified foods to provide essential vitamins and minerals. Small dogs need a variety of vitamins to support various physiological functions, including vitamin A for vision health, vitamin D for bone health, and vitamin E for immune function.

☐ Water: Small dogs need to drink enough water to support healthy digestion, nutrient absorption, and general health. Make sure they always have access to clean, fresh water throughout the day, and keep an eye on how much they're drinking, particularly in hot weather or when they're exercising more.

- Antioxidants: Include foods high in antioxidants, such as berries, spinach, kale, and broccoli, in your dog diet to support their immune system function and general health. Antioxidants, such as vitamin C and E, selenium, and beta-carotene, help combat oxidative stress and shield dog cells from damage caused by free radicals.

- Consider adding probiotic supplements or foods rich in natural probiotics, like yogurt, kefir, and fermented vegetables, to your small dog's diet to support digestive health. Probiotics are beneficial bacteria that support digestive health by maintaining a healthy balance of gut flora.

- Omega-3 Fatty Acids: To support overall health and well-being, include omega-3-rich foods like fatty fish (salmon, mackerel, sardines), flaxseeds, and chia seeds in your dog diet. Omega-3 fatty acids, which are commonly found in fish oil supplements, are good for dogs' skin, coat, joints, and cognitive function. Examples of these fatty acids are EPA (eicosapentaenoic acid) and DHA (docosahexaenoic acid).

Portion Control for Small Dogs

The average dog requires about 30 calories per pound of body weight; naturally, an active dog will require more; small, energetic dogs also require more calories; in addition, you need to consider the dog's condition; my dog, who is older and less active, tends to gain weight, so I feed him a little less to prevent this from happening. Dogs, like people, have varying metabolisms and body compositions. Keep an eye on your dog's weight; if it's increasing, reduce feeding by 10%; if it's decreasing, increase feeding by 10%. Your dog should be lean so that you can SEE a defined waist when you stand sideways. If your dog has a defined waist and you can lightly run your hands over the side and feel the ribs, then he or she is too fat; if the ribs are easily felt and the hip bones protrude, then the dog is too thin. Adjust the amount of food given to the dog based on these observations.

Ingredients to Avoid in Homemade Dog Food

While many foods are safe and beneficial for dogs, there are also several ingredients that should be avoided due to potential health risks or toxicity. This is why it's important to be mindful of the ingredients you use when making homemade dog food in order to ensure that your dog receives a balanced and nutritious diet. A good puppy food should contain the following: enough fat, but not too much; some carbohydrates for energy; enough vitamins and trace minerals to support their growth; and an adequate source of easily digested protein, primarily animal based, since dogs evolved eating animal protein.

The food should taste good, not spoil easily, be made from readily available ingredients, and be inexpensive enough to be affordable. It shouldn't be so calorie-dense that the puppy (especially a large breed) grows too fast, because too much weight on the developing joints can mess them up. In other for you to keep your dog safe and make healthy homemade foods, avoid these ingredients and foods:

- Grapes and Raisins: Grapes and raisins can cause kidney failure in dogs, even in small quantities. It's unclear exactly what makes these fruits toxic to dogs, so it's safest to avoid them entirely.
- Onions and Garlic: Onions and garlic contain compounds that can damage red blood cells and lead to

a condition called hemolytic anemia in dogs. Even small amounts can be toxic for your dog.

- Chocolate: Due to their higher cocoa content, baking and dark chocolate are especially dangerous. Both theobromine and caffeine, which are found in chocolate, are toxic to dogs and can cause symptoms like vomiting, diarrhea, rapid breathing, elevated heart rate, seizures, or even death.
- Xylitol: Often present in sugar-free gum, candies, baked goods, and other products, xylitol is a sugar substitute that can release insulin into the bloodstream too quickly in dogs, resulting in hypoglycemia (low blood sugar), seizures, liver failure, and even death. Make sure products do not contain xylitol by closely reading ingredient labels.
- Avocado: Although ripe avocado flesh is less toxic, it's best to avoid feeding avocados altogether to prevent potential health issues. Avocados contain persin, a toxin

that can cause vomiting, diarrhea, and heart congestion in dogs.

- Alcohol: Whether in the form of alcoholic beverages or foods containing alcohol, alcohol is toxic to dogs and can cause symptoms like vomiting, diarrhea, difficulty breathing, tremors, coma, and death. Keep all alcoholic substances out of reach of pets.
- Macadamia nuts: Macadamia nuts are highly toxic to dogs and can cause symptoms like weakness, lethargy, vomiting, tremors, and hyperthermia. Ingestion of even small amounts can lead to severe illness and require veterinary treatment.
- Caffeine: Caffeine consumption can result in symptoms like seizures, tremors, collapse, and rapid breathing. It is important to keep pets away from caffeinated products and to make sure they do not have access to tea bags or leftover coffee grounds.
- Reduce the amount of fat in your dog's diet because high-fat foods,

like fatty meats, fried foods, and rich dairy products, can upset your dog's stomach and lead to pancreatitis and obesity.

Batch Cooking and Freezing Homemade Dog Food

When you take the time to prepare large batches of homemade dog food and freeze individual portions, you can save time, minimize waste, and give your dog a consistent and balanced diet. Batch cooking and freezing homemade dog food is a great way to streamline meal preparation while ensuring that your dog receives nutritious and delicious meals every day.

Benefits of Batch Cooking and Freezing

1. Making big batches of homemade dog food at once will help you save time when preparing meals for your dog throughout the week.
2. Cooking in larger quantities during batch cooking helps you use up ingredients more effectively and reduce food waste.
3. Freezing individual portions of homemade dog food helps you make sure your dog has a balanced, consistent diet every day.
4. It's simple to defrost and serve the appropriate amount of homemade dog food based on your dog's size and nutritional requirements when it's frozen in individual portions.

Planning and Preparation

Planning your homemade dog food recipes and figuring out what ingredients you'll need is the first step. Take into account your dog's nutritional needs, preferences, and any dietary restrictions or allergies. To ensure you have everything you need for batch cooking, buy high-quality ingredients in bulk and choose recipes that freeze well and portion easily into individual servings. Steer clear of recipes that call for ingredients that might not freeze well or turn mushy when thawed.

Batch Cooking Process

Follow the recommended food safety and hygiene procedures when preparing and cooking your homemade dog food recipes. To accommodate larger batch sizes and ensure even cooking, use slow cookers or large pots and pans. After the homemade dog food is cooked, let it cool completely before portioning and freezing it to prevent the growth of bacteria.

Portioning and Freezing

Use measuring cups or kitchen scales to ensure precise portion sizes, divide the cooled homemade dog food into individual portions according to your dog's size and daily feeding requirements. Transfer each portion of homemade dog food into freezer-safe containers or resealable plastic bags. Make sure to label each one with the contents and date for easy identification. The portioned homemade dog food containers or bags should be placed in the freezer and frozen until solid. Make sure to remove as much air as possible from them to avoid freezer burn and preserve freshness.

Thawing and Serving

When you are ready to serve, take out the desired amount of homemade dog food from the freezer and thaw it in the fridge for a full night or until it is completely thawed. Alternatively, you can use a microwave on low power or submerge the container in a bowl of warm water to thaw individual portions of homemade dog food. After thawing, reheat the homemade dog food to your dog's preferred temperature, if needed, and serve it slightly warm or room temperature. To avoid bacterial growth, throw away any leftover thawed homemade dog food after serving.

Storage and Rotation

Use older batches of homemade dog food first and replenish your supply with freshly batch-cooked meals. Keep a log or inventory of the homemade dog food stored in your freezer to track batch dates and ensure proper rotation. Store the frozen and batch-cooked homemade dog food in the freezer for up to several months, depending on the recipe and ingredients used.

Weekly Meal Planning for Small Dogs

	MORNING 7:30 AM	EVENING 6:30 PM
MONDAY	Tuna and Pasta Salad	Venison and Rice Pilaf
TUESDAY	Lamb and Barley Stew	Duck and Lentil Casserole

WEDNESDAY	Pork and Potato Hash	Bison and Chickpea Curry
THURSDAY	Beef and Spinach Meatballs	Chicken and Barley Soup
FRIDAY	Beef and Barley Bowl	Salmon and Sweet Potato Mash
SATURDAY	Chicken and Chickpea Salad	Chicken and Pumpkin Stew
SUNDAY	Sweet Potato Chews	Duck and Oatmeal Bake

The Recipes Below are designed with the assumption that the weight of an average small dog is 10 pounds. Most of the serving sizes are designed for dogs that weigh this much. Kindly adjust to suit the weight and nutritional requirements of your dog.

Basic Homemade Dog Food Recipes

1. Chicken and Rice

Serving Size: ½ cup

Yield: 3 cups

Ingredients

- 1 cup cooked chicken breast diced
- 1 cup cooked white rice
- 1/2 cup cooked sweet potatoes mashed
- 1/4 cup cooked carrots diced
- 1/4 cup cooked green beans chopped

• 1 tablespoon olive oil

Step by Step Preparations

• Cook the chicken breast until it is fully cooked and dice it into small bite-sized pieces.

• Cook the white rice according to package instructions until it is fluffy and tender.

• Cook the sweet potatoes until it is soft, then mash them until they are smooth.

• Cook the carrots and green beans until they are tender, then dice or chop them into small pieces.

• In a large mixing bowl, combine the cooked chicken breast, cooked white rice, mashed sweet potatoes, diced carrots, diced green beans, and olive oil. Mix them well to combine all ingredients evenly.

• That's it. Your dog food is ready.

Nutritional Information (per serving)
Protein: 20g, Carbohydrates: 25, Fat:8, Fiber:3,
Calories: 280 calories

2. Beef and Sweet Potato Stew

Serving Size: ¼ cup

Yield: 6 cups

Ingredients

- 1 lb lean ground beef

- 2 cups sweet potatoes peeled and diced

- 1 cup carrots diced

- 1 cup green beans chopped

- 3 cups low-sodium beef or chicken broth

- 1 tablespoon olive oil

Step by Step Preparations

• In a large pot, heat olive oil over medium heat. Add ground beef and cook until it is browned. Break it up into small pieces with a spatula.

• Add diced sweet potatoes, carrots, and chopped green beans to the pot. Stir to combine them with the cooked beef.

• Pour in low-sodium beef or chicken broth, ensure that the vegetables and beef are fully submerged in the liquid.

• Bring the mixture to a boil, then reduce heat to low and simmer for about 20-25 minutes or until the vegetables are tender and the flavors have melded together.

• Remove the pot from heat and allow the stew to cool completely before serving it to your dog.

• Portion the beef and sweet potato stew into individual servings based on your dog's weight and dietary needs. For a 10-pound dog, a typical serving size would be 1/2 cup.

•Store any leftover stew in an airtight container in the refrigerator for up to 3-4 days or portion it into freezer-safe containers or resealable bags and freeze for longer storage.

Nutritional Information (per serving):
Protein: 15g, Fat: 8g, Carbohydrates: 20, Fiber: 4g, Calories: 200 kcal

3. Turkey and Quinoa

Serving Size: ¼ cup

Ingredients

•1 cup cooked quinoa

- 1 lb ground turkey
- 1 cup chopped mixed vegetables; carrots, peas, green beans.
- 2 cups low-sodium chicken broth
- 2 tablespoons olive oil
- 1 teaspoon dried parsley

Step by Step Preparations

- In a large skillet, heat olive oil over medium heat. Add ground turkey and cook until it is browned. Break it apart with a spoon as it cooks.
- Add mixed vegetables to the skillet and cook for 5 minutes until vegetables are tender.
- Stir in cooked quinoa and dried parsley if you are using, then pour in chicken broth. Bring the mixture to a simmer and cook for another 5-10 minutes until the broth has been absorbed and the mixture is heated through.

•Remove from heat and let it cool completely before serving.

•Store any leftovers

Nutritional Information (per serving):

Protein: 15g, Fat: 8g, Carbohydrates: 15g, Fiber: 2g, Calories: 180 calories per 1/2 cup serving

---

4. Salmon and Oatmeal

Serving Size: ¼ – ½ cup

Ingredients

•1 cup cooked salmon boneless, skinless

•1 cup cooked oatmeal (cooked in water, no added salt or sugar)

•1/2 cup cooked vegetables like carrots, green beans, or peas

•1 tablespoon olive oil

Step by Step Preparations

• Cook the salmon by baking, grilling, or poaching it until it is fully cooked. Remove any bones and skin, then flake the salmon into small pieces.

• Cook the oatmeal according to package instructions, use water and without adding any salt or sugar.

• Cook the vegetables until tender, then chop them into small pieces.

• In a mixing bowl, combine the cooked salmon, oatmeal, cooked vegetables, and olive oil. Mix them well to combine all ingredients evenly.

• Serve.

Nutritional Information (per serving):

Protein:12g, Fat: 6g, Carbohydrates:15g, Fiber: 2g,
Calories:150 calories per 1/2 cup serving

5. Eggs and Cottage Cheese Scramble

Serving Size: ½ cup

Ingredients

- 2 eggs
- 1/4 cup cottage cheese
- 1 teaspoon olive oil
- 1/4 cup chopped vegetables like spinach, bell peppers, carrots.
- Pinch of dried herbs like parsley or basil.

Step by Step Preparations

- Crack the eggs into a bowl and whisk until well beaten.

• In a non-stick skillet, heat the olive oil over medium heat

• Add the chopped vegetables to the skillet and sauté until they begin to soften about 2-3 minutes.

• Pour the beaten eggs into the skillet and stir gently with a spatula.

• Cook the eggs and stir it occasionally until they are almost set but still slightly runny.

• Add the cottage cheese to the skillet and continue to cook, give it gentle stirring until the eggs are fully cooked and the cottage cheese is heated through.

• Remove the skillet from the heat and sprinkle the dried herbs over the scrambled eggs.

• Allow the scrambled eggs to cool slightly before serving to your small dog.

Nutritional Information:

Calories per serving: 120 kcal, Protein: 10g, Fat: 7g, Carbohydrates: 3g, Fiber: 1gram

6. Tuna and Pasta Salad

Serving Size: 1/4 cup

Ingredients

- •2 eggs
- •1/4 cup cottage cheese
- •1 teaspoon olive oil
- •1/4 cup chopped vegetables such as spinach, bell peppers, or carrots.

Step by Step Preparations

•Crack the eggs into a mixing bowl and whisk until well beaten.

- In a non-stick skillet, heat the olive oil over medium heat

- Pour the beaten eggs into the skillet and cook. Stir it occasionally until they begin to set.

- Add the cottage cheese and chopped vegetables to the skillet and continue to cook until the eggs are fully cooked and the cottage cheese is warmed through.

- Remove the skillet from heat and allow the scramble to cool slightly before serving.

Nutritional Information (per serving):

Calories: 150 kcal, Protein: 14g, Fat: 9g,
Carbohydrates: 2g, Fiber: 0.5g, Calcium: 80 mg

---

7. Lamb and Barley Stew

Serving Size: 6

Ingredients

- 1 lb (450g) lamb meat diced
- 1 cup barley rinsed
- 2 carrots chopped
- 1 cup green bean trimmed and chopped
- 1 sweet potato peeled and diced
- 4 cups low-sodium chicken or beef broth
- 2 tablespoons olive oil

Step by Step Preparations

- In a large pot, heat olive oil over medium heat. Add diced lamb meat and cook until it is browned on all sides about 5 minutes.
- Add barley to the pot and stir to coat in the oil and lamb drippings. Cook for 2 minutes.
- Pour chicken or beef broth into the pot and bring to a boil. Reduce heat to low and simmer for 20 minutes.

- Add chopped carrots, green beans, and sweet potato to the pot. Continue simmering for 20-25 minutes or until the vegetables are tender and the barley is cooked through.
- Remove the pot from heat and allow the stew to cool before serving

---

Nutritional Information (per serving):

Calories: 320 kcal, Protein: 22g, Fat: 12g, Carbohydrates: 30g, Fiber: 6g

---

8. Pork and Potato Hash

Serving Size: ¼ cup for 5–10 lbs dog, ½ ,cup for 10–15 lbs.

Yield: 2 cups

Ingredients

- 1 cup cooked lean pork diced

- 1 cup cooked sweet potatoes mashed
- 1/2 cup cooked peas
- 1/2 cup cooked carrots diced
- 1 tablespoon olive oil

Step by Step Preparations

- In a large skillet, heat olive oil over medium heat.
- Add diced pork to the skillet and cook until it is browned and cooked through.
- Add mashed sweet potatoes, cooked peas, and diced carrots to the skillet. Stir it well to combine.
- Cook for 5 minutes, stir until all ingredients are heated through and well combined.
- Remove from heat and allow to cool before serving.

Nutritional Information (per 1/4 cup serving):

Protein: 8, Fat: 4g, Carbohydrates: 12g, Fiber: 2g,
Calories: 110

9. Venison and Rice Pilaf

Serving Size: ½ cup

Yield: 4 cups

Ingredients

- 1 cup venison ground or diced
- 1 cup brown rice uncooked
- 2 cups low-sodium chicken broth
- 1 cup chopped mixed vegetables like carrots, peas, green beans.
- 1 tablespoon olive oil

Step by Step Preparations

- In a large saucepan, heat the olive oil over medium heat. Add the venison and cook until it is browned. Break it apart with a spoon as it cooks.

•Add the uncooked brown rice to the saucepan and stir to combine with the venison.

•Pour in the chicken broth and bring the mixture to a boil. Reduce the heat to low, cover it, and simmer for about 30-40 minutes or until the rice is cooked and the liquid is absorbed.

•Stir in the chopped mixed vegetables and continue to cook for 5-10 minutes or until the vegetables are tender.

•Remove the saucepan from the heat and let the pilaf cool completely before serving.

Nutritional Information (per serving):

Calories: 150 kcal, Protein: 10g, Fat: 5g, Carbohydrates: 15g, Fiber: 2g

---

10. Duck and Lentil Casserole

Serving Size: ½ cup

Yield: 4 cups

Ingredients

- 1 cup cooked duck meat shredded
- 1 cup cooked lentils
- 1/2 cup cooked brown rice
- 1/2 cup diced carrots
- 1/2 cup diced sweet potatoes
- 1/4 cup chopped parsley
- 2 cups low-sodium chicken or vegetable broth
- 2 tablespoons olive oil

Step by Step Preparations

- Preheat your oven to 350°F (175°C).
- In a large mixing bowl, combine the cooked duck meat, lentils, brown rice, diced carrots, diced sweet potatoes, and chopped parsley.

- Pour the low-sodium chicken or vegetable broth and olive oil over the ingredients and mix until they are well combined.

- Transfer the mixture to a greased casserole dish and spread it out evenly.

- Cover the casserole dish with aluminum foil and bake in the preheated oven for 25-30 minutes or until the vegetables are tender.

- Allow the casserole to cool completely before serving it.

Nutritional Information (per 1/2 cup serving):

Calories: 150 kcal, Protein: 10g, Fat: 5g, Carbohydrates: 15g, Fiber: 3g

---

11. Bison and Chickpea Curry

Serving Size: ½ cup

Yield: 4 cups

Ingredients

- 1 cup cooked buffalo meat diced
- 1 cup cooked chickpeas (garbanzo beans) drained and rinsed
- 1/2 cup cooked brown rice
- 1/2 cup diced carrots
- 1/2 cup diced sweet potatoes
- 1/4 cup diced green beans
- 2 cups low-sodium beef or vegetable broth
- 1 tablespoon coconut oil
- 1 teaspoon turmeric powder
- 1/2 teaspoon ground ginger
- 1/2 teaspoon ground cinnamon

Step by Step Preparations

- In a large pot, heat coconut oil over medium heat. Add diced carrots, sweet potatoes, and green beans. Cook for 5-7 minutes until vegetables are slightly softened.

•Add diced buffalo meat and cooked chickpeas to the pot. Stir to combine with the vegetables.

•Pour in the low-sodium beef or vegetable broth along with turmeric powder, ground ginger, and ground cinnamon. Stir well to allow the spices blend together with the food.

•Add cooked brown rice to the pot and stir again. Bring the mixture to a simmer, then reduce heat to low and cover. Let the curry simmer for 15-20 minutes. Allow the flavors to meld together and the vegetables to become tender.

•Once the curry is cooked through and the vegetables are tender, remove from heat and let it cool before you serve.

Nutritional Information (per 1/2 cup serving):

Calories: 150 kcal, Protein: 8g, Fat: 4g, Carbohydrates: 20g, Fiber: 4g, Calcium: 20mg, Iron: 1.5mg

12. Vegetable and Tofu Stir-Fry

Serving Size: ½ cup

Yield: 2 cups

Ingredients

- 1 cup firm tofu diced into small cubes
- 1/2 cup thinly sliced mixed vegetables such as carrots, peas, green beans.
- 1/4 cup cooked brown rice
- 1 tablespoon olive oil
- 1/2 teaspoon minced garlic
- 1/4 teaspoon grated ginger
- 1 tablespoon low-sodium soy sauce
- 1 tablespoon chopped fresh parsley

Step by Step Preparations

•Heat the olive oil in a skillet or wok over medium heat. Add the diced tofu cubes and cook until it is lightly browned on all sides about 5-7 minutes. Remove the tofu from the skillet and set aside.

•In the same skillet, add the mixed vegetables and sauté until tender-crisp about 3-5 minutes.

•If using garlic and ginger, add them to the skillet and sauté for 1-2 minutes until fragrant.

•Return the cooked tofu to the skillet and add the cooked brown rice. Stir to combine.

•If using soy sauce, drizzle it over the tofu and vegetable mixture and toss to coat evenly. Cook for another 1-2 minutes to allow the flavors to meld.

•Remove the skillet from heat and let the stir-fry cool to room temperature before serving it to your dog.

Nutritional Information:

Calories per serving: 100 kcal, Protein: 5g, Fat: 4g, Carbohydrates: 10g, Fiber: 2g, Calcium: 50mg, Iron: 1mg

13. Turkey and Pumpkin Chili

Serving Size: ¼ cup

Yield 16

Ingredients

- 1 lb lean ground turkey
- 1 cup canned pumpkin puree (not pumpkin pie filling)
- 1 cup cooked brown rice
- 1/2 cup diced carrots
- 1/2 cup diced zucchini
- 1/2 cup diced bell peppers

- 4 cups low-sodium chicken broth

- 1 tablespoon olive oil

Step by Step Preparations

- In a large pot, heat olive oil over medium heat. Add ground turkey and cook until it is browned. Break it up with a spoon as it cooks.

- Add diced carrots, zucchini, and bell peppers to the pot. Cook for 5 minutes until vegetables are slightly softened.

- Stir in canned pumpkin puree and cooked brown rice until well combined.

- Pour in chicken broth and bring the mixture to a simmer. Reduce heat to low and let the chili cook for 20-25 minutes, allow flavors to meld together.

- Remove from heat and let the chili cool completely before serving..

Nutritional Information (per serving):

Calories: 60 kcal, Protein: 5.5g, Fat: 2g,
Carbohydrates: 4g, Fiber: 1.5g, Calcium: 10mg,
Phosphorus: 45mg, Sodium: 40mg

14. Chicken and Barley Soup

Serving Size: ½ cup

Yield 8

Ingredients

- 1 cup cooked chicken breast diced
- 1/2 cup barley rinsed
- 1 carrot, chopped
- 1/2 cup green beans chopped
- 4 cups low-sodium chicken broth
- 2 cups water
- 1 tablespoon olive oil

Step by Step Preparations

• In a large pot, heat olive oil over medium heat. Add diced chicken breast and cook until lightly browned.

• Add barley, chopped carrot, and green beans to the pot. Stir it to combine.

• Pour in chicken broth and water, and bring the mixture to a boil.

• Reduce heat to low, cover, and simmer for about 45 minutes or until barley is tender and soup has thickened.

• Allow the soup to cool completely before serving..

Nutritional Information (per serving):

Calories: 100 kcal, Protein: 8g, Fat: 3g, Carbohydrates: 10g, Fiber: 2 g

---

15. Beef and Spinach Meatballs

Serving Size: 2-3 Meatballs

Yield: 12-15 Meatballs

Ingredients

- 1 pound lean ground beef
- 1 cup fresh spinach chopped
- 1/2 cup cooked brown rice
- 1/4 cup carrots grated
- 1 egg
- 2 tablespoons parsley chopped
- 1 tablespoon olive oil

Step by Step Preparations

- Preheat your oven to 350°F (175°C) and line a baking sheet with parchment paper.

●In a large mixing bowl, combine the ground beef, chopped spinach, cooked brown rice, grated carrots, egg, chopped parsley, and olive oil. Mix them well until all ingredients blends perfectly.

●Roll the mixture into small meatballs, about the size of a tablespoon, and place them on the prepared baking sheet.

●Bake the meatballs in the preheated oven for 15-20 minutes or until cooked through and lightly browned.

●Remove the meatballs from the oven and let them cool completely before serving.

Nutritional Information (per serving of 3 meatballs):

Calories: 120 kcal, Protein: 12g, Fat: 6g, Carbohydrates: 4g, Fiber: 1gram, Calcium: 10 mg, Iron: 1 mg

---

16. Salmon and Potato Cakes

Serving Size: 1

Yield: 8–10

Ingredients

- 1 cup cooked salmon flaked
- 1 cup cooked mashed potatoes
- 1/2 cup cooked peas mashed
- 1/4 cup grated carrot
- 1 tablespoon chopped parsley
- 1 egg, beaten
- 2 tablespoons olive oil

Step by Step Preparations

- In a large mixing bowl, combine the cooked salmon, mashed potatoes, mashed peas, grated carrot, chopped parsley, and beaten egg. Mix them well until all ingredients are evenly distributed.

•Divide the mixture into small portions and shape them into patties or cakes.

•Heat the olive oil in a skillet over medium heat. Once hot, add the salmon and potato cakes and cook for 3-4 minutes on each side or until golden brown and heated through.

•Remove the cooked salmon and potato cakes from the skillet and allow them to cool slightly before serving.

Nutritional Information (per serving):

Calories: 100, Protein: 8g, Fat: 5g, Carbohydrates: 5g, Fiber: 1g, Calcium: 20mg, Iron: 1mg

---

17. Tuna and Carrot Muffins

Serving Size: 1

Ingredients

- 1 can (5 ounces) of tuna in water drained
- 1 cup grated carrots
- 1 cup whole wheat flour
- 1 teaspoon baking powder
- 2 eggs
- 1/4 cup plain Greek yogurt
- 1/4 cup water

Step by Step Preparations

- Preheat your oven to 350°F (175°C) and grease a muffin tin or line with paper liners.
- In a large mixing bowl, combine the drained tuna, grated carrots, whole wheat flour, and baking powder. Stir until they are well combined.

- In a separate bowl, beat the eggs lightly, then add them to the tuna and carrot mixture.

- Add the plain Greek yogurt and water to the bowl, and mix until all ingredients are thoroughly combined.

- Spoon the batter evenly into the prepared muffin tin. Fill each cup about two-thirds full.

- Bake the muffins in the preheated oven for 20-25 minutes or until a toothpick inserted into the center comes out clean.

- Remove the muffins from the oven and allow them to cool completely before serving.

Nutritional Information (per muffin):

Calories: 75, Protein: 5g, Fat: 2g, Carbohydrates: 9g, Fiber: 1g

---

18. Lamb and Rice Balls

Serving Size: 1

Yield: 20 balls

Ingredients

- 1 pound ground lamb
- 1 cup cooked brown rice
- 1/2 cup finely chopped spinach
- 1/4 cup grated carrot
- 1/4 cup finely chopped parsley
- 1 egg
- 2 tablespoons olive oil

Step by Step Preparations

- Preheat your oven to 350°F (175°C) and line a baking sheet with parchment paper.
- In a large mixing bowl, combine the ground lamb, cooked brown rice, chopped spinach, grated carrot, chopped parsley, egg, and olive

oil. Mix them well until all ingredients are evenly combined.

•Roll the mixture into small balls, about the size of a tablespoon and place them on the prepared baking sheet.

•Bake the lamb and rice balls in the preheated oven for 20-25 minutes or until it is cooked through and lightly browned.

•Allow the balls to cool completely before serving. Store any leftovers.

Nutritional Information (per serving):

Calories: 60 kcal, Protein: 4g, Fat: 4g, Carbohydrates: 2 g, Fiber: 1g, Calcium: 5mg, Iron: 0.5mg, Sodium: 10mg

---

19. Turkey and Cranberry Biscuits

Serving Size: 1

Ingredients

- 1 cup cooked turkey shredded
- 1/2 cup cooked brown rice
- 1/4 cup dried cranberries chopped
- 1/4 cup unsweetened applesauce
- 1 egg
- 1 tablespoon olive oil

Step by Step Preparations

- Preheat your oven to 350°F (175°C) and line a baking sheet with parchment paper.
- In a large mixing bowl, combine the cooked turkey, cooked brown rice, chopped dried cranberries, unsweetened applesauce, egg, and olive oil. Mix well until all ingredients are evenly combined.

• Scoop tablespoon-sized portions of the mixture and shape them into small biscuits using your hands. Place the biscuits onto the prepared baking sheet. Leave some space between each one.

• Bake the biscuits in the preheated oven for 15-20 minutes or until they are golden brown and firm to the touch.

• Remove the biscuits from the oven and allow them to cool completely on a wire rack before serving to your dog.

Nutritional Information (per biscuit):

Calories: 45 kcal, Protein: 3g, Fat: 2g, Carbohydrates: 5g, Fiber: 1 gram, Calcium: 5mg, Iron: 0.3 mg

---

20.Chicken and Cheese Omelette

Serving Size: 1 small omelet

Yield: 1

Ingredients

- 1/4 cup cooked chicken breast shredded
- 1 egg
- 1 tablespoon shredded cheese (cheddar or mozzarella)
- 1 teaspoon olive oil

Step by Step Preparations

- In a small bowl, whisk the egg until well beaten.
- Heat the olive oil in a non-stick skillet over medium heat.
- Pour the beaten egg into the skillet and allow it to cook for 1-2 minutes until it starts to set around the edges.

- Sprinkle the shredded chicken evenly over the egg.

- Sprinkle the shredded cheese evenly over the chicken.

- Gently fold one side of the omelet over the filling to create a half-moon shape.

- Cook for 1-2 minutes until the cheese is melted and the omelet is cooked through.

- Remove from heat and allow to cool slightly before serving.

Nutritional Information (per serving):

Calories: 130 kcal, Protein: 13g, Fat: 8g, Carbohydrates:1 gram, Fiber: 0g, Calcium: 60mg, Iron: 1mg

---

Homemade Hypoallergenic Dog Recipes

It can be a little challenging to make allergy food for dogs, but it is definitely possible. To begin with, you should identify the ingredient or ingredients that your dog is allergic to so that you can avoid using them in the recipe. After you have determined which ingredients are safe for your dog, you can look into different recipes and safe ingredient combinations. As you are currently preparing your own dog food from scratch with whole, fresh ingredients, you have complete control over the ingredients and can guarantee that no allergens are included.

21. Turkey and Sweet Potato Stew

Serving Size: 1 cup

Yield: 8

Ingredients

- 1 pound lean ground turkey

- 2 cups sweet potatoes peeled and diced

- 1 cup carrots diced

- 1 cup green beans chopped

- 4 cups low-sodium chicken or vegetable broth

- 2 tablespoons olive oil

Step by Step Preparations

- In a large pot, heat the olive oil over medium heat. Add the ground turkey and cook until it is browned. Break it apart with a spoon as it cooks.

• Add the diced sweet potatoes, carrots, and green beans to the pot. Stir to combine with the cooked turkey.

• Pour in the chicken or vegetable broth. Ensure that the ingredients are fully submerged. Bring the mixture to a boil.

• Reduce the heat to low and simmer the stew for about 20-25 minutes or until the sweet potatoes and carrots are tender.

• Once the stew is cooked, remove it from the heat and allow it to cool slightly.

• Use a ladle to portion the stew into individual serving sizes suitable for your dog's weight and appetite.

Nutritional Information (per serving):

Calories: 180 kcal, Protein: 15g, Fat: 6g, Carbohydrates: 15g, Fiber: 3g, Calcium: 30mg, Iron: 2mg, Sodium: 50mg

---

22. Salmon and Rice

Serving Size: ½ cup

Yield: 4 cups

Ingredients

- 2 cups cooked brown rice
- 1 cup cooked salmon flaked
- 1/2 cup cooked carrots diced
- 1/2 cup cooked green beans chopped
- 2 tablespoons olive oil

Step by Step Preparations

- Cook the brown rice according to package instructions until it is tender. Set aside to cool.
- Cook the salmon by boiling, steaming, or baking until fully cooked. Remove any bones and flake the salmon into small pieces.
- Cook the carrots and green beans until tender, then dice and chop them into small pieces.
- In a large mixing bowl, combine the cooked rice, flaked salmon, diced carrots, chopped green beans, and olive oil. Mix well to blend all ingredients evenly.
- That's it. Dog food is set.

Nutritional Information (per serving):

Calories: 200 kcal, Protein: 10g, Fat: 8g, Carbohydrates: 22g, Fiber: 3g

---

23. Lamb and Quinoa Casserole

Serving Size: ½ **cup**

Yield: 6

Ingredients

- 1 cup quinoa rinsed
- 1 pound ground lamb
- 1 cup carrots diced
- 1 cup green beans chopped
- 1/2 cup peas
- 4 cups low-sodium chicken or vegetable broth
- 2 tablespoons olive oil

Step by Step Preparations

- Preheat the oven to 350°F (175°C). Grease a casserole dish with olive oil and set aside.
- In a large skillet, heat the olive oil over medium heat. Add the ground lamb and cook

until it is browned. Break it apart with a spoon as it cooks.

•Add the diced carrots and chopped green beans to the skillet with the ground lamb. Cook for 5 minutes until the vegetables start to soften.

•In a separate saucepan, bring the chicken or vegetable broth to a boil. Add the rinsed quinoa to the boiling broth and reduce the heat to low. Simmer for 15 minutes until the quinoa is cooked and the liquid is absorbed.

•Combine the cooked quinoa with the lamb and vegetable mixture in the skillet. Stir to mix well.

•Transfer the mixture to the greased casserole dish and spread it out evenly.

•Bake in the preheated oven for 20-25 minutes until the casserole is heated through and the top is lightly browned.

•Remove from the oven and let cool slightly before serving.

Nutritional Information (per serving):

Calories: 250, Protein: 15g, Fat: 10g, Carbohydrates: 25g, Fiber: 4g, Calcium: 30mg, Iron: 2mg, Potassium: 300mg

---

24. Venison and Potato Mash

Serving Size: ½ cup

Yield: 6 cups

Ingredients

• 1 lb venison meat cooked and diced

• 2 medium potatoes peeled and diced

• 1 cup green beans chopped

• 1 cup carrots diced

•1 tablespoon olive oil

•4 cups water or low-sodium vegetable broth

Step by Step Preparations

•In a large pot, bring water or vegetable broth to a boil.

•Add diced potatoes to the boiling liquid and cook until tender about 10-15 minutes.

•In a separate pan, heat olive oil over medium heat and add diced venison meat. Cook until browned and fully cooked through.

•Once the potatoes are cooked, drain excess liquid and mash them using a potato masher or fork.

•Add cooked venison meat, chopped green beans, and diced carrots to the mashed potatoes.

•Mix all ingredients together until well combined.

- Allow the mixture to cool before serving it to your dog.
- Store any leftovers.

Nutritional Information (per serving):

Calories: 150 kcal, Protein: 10g, Fat: 6g, Carbohydrates: 12g, Fiber: 2g, Calcium: 20mg, Iron: 1mg

---

25. Duck and Oatmeal Bake

Serving Size: ¼ cup

Yield: 16 servings (4 cups)

Ingredients

- 1 pound ground duck meat
- 2 cups cooked oatmeal

- 1/2 cup cooked peas
- 1/2 cup cooked carrots, diced
- 1/4 cup chopped parsley (optional, for added flavor)
- 2 tablespoons olive oil
- 1 egg, beaten

Step by Step Preparations

- Preheat your oven to 350°F (175°C). Grease a baking dish or line it with parchment paper for easy cleanup.
- In a large mixing bowl, combine the ground duck meat, cooked oatmeal, cooked peas, cooked carrots, chopped parsley, olive oil, and beaten egg. Mix until well combined.
- Transfer the mixture to the prepared baking dish and spread it evenly.
- Bake in the preheated oven for 25-30 minutes or until the top is golden brown and the edges are crispy.

- Remove from the oven and allow it to cool completely before serving.

- Once cooled, cut the duck and oatmeal into small bite-sized pieces suitable for your small dog's size.

Nutritional Information (per serving):

Calories: 150 kcal, Protein: 10g, Fat: 8g, Carbohydrates: 10g, Fiber: 2g, Calcium: 20mg, Iron: 1mg

---

26. Chicken and Pumpkin Stew

Serving Size: ½ cup

Yield: 8

Ingredients

- 1 lb boneless skinless chicken breast or thighs diced
- 1 cup canned pure pumpkin (not pumpkin pie filling)
- 1 cup cooked brown rice or quinoa
- 1 cup diced carrots
- 1 cup diced sweet potatoes
- 4 cups low-sodium chicken broth
- 2 tablespoons olive oil

Step by Step Preparations

- In a large pot, heat the olive oil over medium heat. Add the diced chicken and cook until browned on all sides about 5-7 minutes.
- Add the diced carrots and sweet potatoes to the pot and cook for 5 minutes. Stir occasionally.
- Pour in the chicken broth and bring the mixture to a boil. Reduce the heat to low and

simmer for 20-25 minutes or until the vegetables are tender and the chicken is cooked through.

- Stir in the canned pumpkin and cooked brown rice or quinoa. Simmer for 5 minutes to allow the flavors to meld together.

- Remove the pot from the heat and let the stew cool to room temperature before serving it to your dog.

Nutritional Information (per serving):

Calories: 150,Protein: 12g, Fat: 6g, Carbohydrates: 12g, Fiber: 2g, Calcium: 20mg, Iron: 1mg, Potassium: 250mg, Sodium: 50mg

---

27. Beef and Barley Bowl

Serving Size: 2

Yield: 2 cups

Ingredients

- 1 cup cooked lean ground beef

- 1/2 cup cooked barley

- 1/4 cup cooked peas

- 1/4 cup cooked carrots diced

- 1 tablespoon olive oil

Step by Step Preparations

- Cook the lean ground beef in a skillet over medium heat until fully cooked. Drain any excess fat and set aside to cool.

- In a separate pot, cook the barley according to package instructions until tender. Drain any excess water and set aside to cool.

- Cook the peas and diced carrots until tender. Drain and set aside to cool..

- In a large mixing bowl, combine the cooked ground beef, barley, peas, carrots, and olive oil. Mix well to ensure all ingredients are evenly distributed. Serve

---

Nutritional Information (per serving):

Calories: 250 kcal, Protein: 20g, Fat: 10g, Carbohydrates: 20g, Fiber: 5g, Calcium: 20mg ,Iron: 2mg

---

28. Rabbit and Pea Risotto

Serving Size: ¼ – ⅓ cup

Yield: 4

Ingredients

- 1 cup Arborio rice
- 2 cups low-sodium chicken broth
- 1 cup cooked rabbit meat, diced
- 1/2 cup peas, fresh or frozen
- 1 tablespoon olive oil
- 1/4 teaspoon dried rosemary
- 1/4 teaspoon dried parsley

Step by Step Preparations

- In a medium saucepan, heat the olive oil over medium heat. Add the Arborio rice and cook. Stir frequently for 2-3 minutes until lightly toasted.
- Gradually add the chicken broth to the saucepan, 1/2 cup at a time. Stir continuously. Allow the liquid to absorb before adding more broth. Cook the rice for about 20 minutes until it is tender and creamy.

• Stir in the cooked rabbit meat and peas, and continue to cook for 5 minutes until the rabbit is heated through and the peas are tender.

• If desired, add the dried rosemary and parsley for added flavor. Remove the risotto from heat and let it cool slightly before serving.

Nutritional Information (per serving):

Calories: 150-200 kcal, Protein: 10-12g, Fat: 5-7g, Carbohydrates: 15-20g, Fiber: 2-3g

---

29. Turkey and Millet

Serving Size: ¼ – ½ cup

Yield: 4

Ingredients

• 1 cup cooked ground turkey

• 1/2 cup cooked millet

- 1/4 cup cooked sweet potatoes mashed
- 1/4 cup cooked carrots diced
- 1 tablespoon olive oil
- 1/4 teaspoon salt, optional.
- 1/4 teaspoon dried parsley

Step by Step Preparations

- Cook ground turkey in a skillet over medium heat until fully cooked. Drain any excess fat and set aside to cool.
- Cook millet according to package instructions until tender. Allow to cool.
- In a large mixing bowl, combine cooked ground turkey, cooked millet, mashed sweet potatoes, diced carrots, olive oil, and salt (if using). Mix well to combine.
- Divide the mixture into individual servings based on your dog's weight and portion

requirements. You can use a measuring cup or kitchen scale to ensure accurate portioning.

Nutritional Information (per serving):

Calories: 150 calorie, Protein: 10, Fat: 6g, Carbohydrates: 15g, Fiber: 2g

---

30. Pork and Potato Mash-Up

Serving Size: ½ cup

Yield: 4 cups

Ingredients

- 1 cup lean ground pork
- 1 cup cooked mashed sweet potatoes
- 1/2 cup cooked mashed white potatoes
- 1/4 cup cooked peas
- 1 tablespoon olive oil

Step by Step Preparations

•In a skillet, cook the lean ground pork over medium heat until fully cooked and no longer pink. Drain any excess fat and set aside to cool.

•In a large bowl, combine the cooked mashed sweet potatoes and white potatoes.

•Add the cooked ground pork to the mashed potatoes and mix well to combine.

•Stir in the cooked peas for added fiber and nutrients.

•Drizzle the olive oil over the pork and potato mixture and mix thoroughly.

Nutritional Information (per serving):

Calories: 200, Protein: 15g, Fat: 8g, Carbohydrates: 15g, Fiber: 2g, Calcium: 10mg, Iron: 1.5mg, Potassium: 200mg, Sodium: 30mg

---

Homemade Dog Recipes for Weight Management

31. Turkey and Vegetable Stew

Serving Size: ¼ cup

Yield: 6 cups

Ingredients

- 1 lb lean ground turkey
- 1 cup chopped carrots
- 1 cup chopped green beans
- 1 cup chopped zucchini
- 1 cup chopped spinach

- 4 cups low-sodium chicken broth

- 1 tablespoon olive oil

Step by Step Preparations

- In a large pot or Dutch oven, heat the olive oil over medium heat. Add the ground turkey and cook until it is browned. Break it apart with a spoon as it cooks.

- Add the chopped carrots, green beans, zucchini, and spinach to the pot. Cook for 5 minutes. Stir occasionally until the vegetables start to soften.

- Pour in the low-sodium chicken broth and bring the mixture to a simmer. Reduce the heat to low and let the stew simmer for 20-25 minutes or until the vegetables are tender and the flavors have melded together.

- Remove the pot from the heat and let the stew cool to room temperature.

Nutritional Information (per 1/4 cup serving):

Calories: 35, Protein: 4g, Fat: 1g, Carbohydrates: 2g,
Fiber: 1g, Calcium: 10mg, Iron: 0.5mg

32. Chicken and Brown Rice Casserole

Serving Size: ½ cup

Yield: 8

Ingredients

- 2 boneless skinless chicken breasts diced
- 1 cup brown rice uncooked
- 1 cup diced carrots
- 1 cup diced green beans
- 4 cups low-sodium chicken broth
- 2 tablespoons olive oil

Step by Step Preparations

- Preheat your oven to 350°F (175°C).

- In a large skillet, heat the olive oil over medium heat. Add the diced chicken breasts and cook until browned on all sides about 5-7 minutes.

- In a separate saucepan, bring the chicken broth to a boil. Add the brown rice, diced carrots, and green beans. Reduce heat to low, cover, and simmer for 20-25 minutes or until the rice is cooked and the vegetables are tender.

- In a large mixing bowl, combine the cooked chicken, rice, and vegetables. Mix well to evenly distribute the ingredients.

- Transfer the mixture to a greased casserole dish and spread it out evenly.

- Cover the casserole dish with aluminum foil and bake in the preheated oven for 25-30 minutes or until heated through.

- Allow the casserole to cool slightly before serving.

Nutritional Information (per serving):

Calories: 150, Protein: 12g, Fat: 5g, Carbohydrates: 13g, Fiber: 2g, Calcium: 20mg, Iron: 1mg

---

33. Fish and Quinoa

Serving Size: ½ cup

Yield: 6 cups

Ingredients

- 1 cup quinoa
- 2 cups low-sodium chicken or vegetable broth

- 1 tablespoon olive oil
- 1 pound white fish filets such as cod, tilapia, or sole cut into bite-sized pieces
- 1 cup chopped mixed vegetables like carrots, peas, and green beans
- 2 tablespoons chopped fresh parsley

Step by Step Preparations

- Rinse the quinoa under cold water to remove any bitterness. In a medium saucepan, combine the quinoa and chicken or vegetable broth. Bring to a boil, then reduce heat to low, cover, and simmer for 15-20 minutes or until the quinoa is cooked and fluffy. Remove from heat and let it cool slightly.
- In a large skillet, heat the olive oil over medium heat. Add the fish filets and cook for 3-4 minutes on each side or until cooked through

and flaky. Remove the fish from the skillet and set aside.

•In the same skillet, add the mixed vegetables and cook for 5-7 minutes or until tender-crisp.

•Add the cooked quinoa and fish to the skillet with the vegetables. Gently toss to combine and heat through.

•Remove from heat and sprinkle with chopped parsley.

Nutritional Information (per 1/2 cup serving):

Calories: 150, Protein: 15g, Fat: 5g, Carbohydrates: 10g, Fiber: 2g, Calcium: 20mg, Iron: 1.5mg, Potassium: 200mg, Sodium: 50mg

---

34. Turkey and Pumpkin Patties

Serving Size: 1

Yield: 8-10

Ingredients

- 1 lb lean ground turkey
- 1 cup canned pumpkin (not pumpkin pie filling)
- 1/2 cup cooked quinoa or brown rice
- 1/4 cup finely chopped spinach
- 1/4 cup finely chopped carrots
- 1 egg
- 1 tablespoon olive oil

Step by Step Preparations

- Preheat your oven to 350°F (175°C) and line a baking sheet with parchment paper.
- In a large mixing bowl, combine the ground turkey, canned pumpkin, cooked quinoa or brown rice, chopped spinach, chopped carrots, egg, and olive oil. Mix well until all ingredients are evenly combined.

•Divide the mixture into equal portions and shape them into patties of your desired size. Place the patties onto the prepared baking sheet.

•Bake the patties in the preheated oven for 25-30 minutes or until cooked through and golden brown on the outside.

•Remove the patties from the oven and allow them to cool completely before serving to your dog.

Nutritional Information (per serving):

Calories: 120 calories per patty, Protein: 10 g, Fat: 6 g, Carbohydrates: 6 g, Fiber: 1.5 g, Calcium: 10 mg, Iron: 1 mg

---

35. Beef and Barley Stew

Serving Size: ½ cup

Yield: 6-8

Ingredients

- 1 lb lean ground beef
- 1 cup barley
- 2 carrots, chopped
- 1 cup green beans chopped
- 1 cup spinach chopped
- 4 cups low-sodium beef or chicken broth
- 2 cloves garlic minced
- 1 tablespoon olive oil

Step by Step Preparations

- In a large pot or Dutch oven, heat olive oil over medium heat. Add minced garlic and cook for 1-2 minutes until fragrant
- Add lean ground beef to the pot and cook until browned. Break it up with a spoon as it cooks.

- Add chopped carrots, green beans, and spinach to the pot and cook for 3-4 minutes until vegetables begin to soften.
- Pour in low-sodium beef or chicken broth and add barley to the pot. Stir well to combine.
- Bring the stew to a boil, then reduce heat to low and let simmer for 45-50 minutes or until the barley is tender and the stew has thickened.
- Allow the stew to cool completely before serving.

Nutritional Information (per serving):

Calories: 150, Protein: 10 g, Fat: 5 g, Carbohydrates: 15 g, Fiber: 3 g, Calcium: 20 mg, Iron: 1 mg

---

36. Chicken and Lentil Soup

Serving Size: 1

Yield: 6-8

Ingredients

- 1 cup dried green lentils
- 2 boneless skinless chicken breasts diced
- 2 carrots diced
- 2 celery stalks diced
- 1 sweet potato diced
- 6 cups low-sodium chicken broth
- 2 cups water
- 1 tablespoon olive oil
- 2 cloves garlic minced
- 1 teaspoon dried thyme
- 1 teaspoon dried parsley
- Salt and pepper to taste

Step by Step Preparations

- Rinse the lentils under cold water and drain.

- In a large pot, heat the olive oil over medium heat. Add the diced chicken breasts and cook until browned on all sides about 5 minutes.
- Add the minced garlic, diced carrots, celery, and sweet potato to the pot. Cook for an additional 5 minutes while stirring occasionally.
- Pour in the chicken broth and water, then add the rinsed lentils, dried thyme, dried parsley, salt, and pepper. Stir to combine.
- Bring the soup to a boil, then reduce the heat to low. Cover and simmer for 45 minutes to 1 hour or until the lentils and vegetables are tender.
- Once the soup is cooked, remove it from the heat and allow it to cool slightly.
- Using an immersion blender or food processor, puree the soup until smooth or to your desired consistency.
- Let the soup cool completely before serving.

Nutritional Information (per 1 cup serving):

Calories: 150-200 kcal, Protein: 15-20 g, Fat: 3-5 g,
Carbohydrates: 15-20 g, Fiber: 5-7 g, Calcium: 20-30
mg, Iron: 2-4 mg

37. Turkey and Vegetable Stir-Fry

Serving Size: ½ cup

Yield: 4

Ingredients

- 1 cup lean ground turkey
- 1/2 cup chopped carrots
- 1/2 cup chopped green beans
- 1/2 cup chopped broccoli
- 1/4 cup chopped bell pepper
- 1/4 cup chopped zucchini
- 1 tablespoon olive oil

- 1 teaspoon minced garlic

- 1/2 teaspoon ground turmeric

- 1 cup cooked brown rice

Step by Step Preparations

- Heat olive oil in a large skillet over medium heat. Add minced garlic and cook for 1-2 minutes until fragrant.

- Add lean ground turkey to the skillet and cook until browned. Break it up with a spatula as it cooks.

- Add chopped carrots, green beans, broccoli, bell pepper, and zucchini to the skillet. Stir-fry for 5-7 minutes until the vegetables are tender-crisp.

- If using ground turmeric, sprinkle it over the stir-fry and mix well to blend together.

●Remove the skillet from heat and let the turkey and vegetable stir-fry cool to room temperature.

Nutritional Information (per serving):

Calories: 120 kcal, Protein: 12g, Fat: 6g, Carbohydrates: 5g, Fiber: 2g

38. Salmon and Sweet Potato Mash

Serving Size: ¼ – ½ cup

Yield: 2–3 cups

Ingredients

●1 cup cooked salmon skinless and boneless

●1 cup cooked sweet potatoes mashed

●1/2 cup cooked green beans chopped

●1/4 cup cooked carrots diced

•2 tablespoons olive oil

Step by Step Preparations

•Cook the salmon by baking, boiling, or grilling until fully cooked. Remove any skin and bones, then flake the salmon into small pieces.

•Cook the sweet potatoes by boiling or roasting until tender. Mash the sweet potatoes using a fork or potato masher until smooth.

•Cook the green beans and carrots until tender, then chop or dice them into small pieces.

•In a mixing bowl, combine the cooked salmon, mashed sweet potatoes, chopped green beans, diced carrots, and olive oil. Mix well to combine all ingredients evenly.

•Divide the mixture into individual servings based on your dog's weight and nutritional needs. Use the serving size guide above to determine the appropriate portion size for your dog.

Nutritional Information (per 1/2 cup serving):

Calories: 150 kcal, Protein: 10g, Fat: 8g, Carbohydrates: 10g, Fiber: 2g, Calcium: 15 mg, Phosphorus: 120 mg, Potassium: 200 mg, Sodium: 50 mg

39. Chicken and Chickpea Salad

Serving Size: ½ cup

Yield: 4

Ingredients

- 1 cup cooked chicken breast diced
- 1 cup cooked chickpeas (garbanzo beans) rinsed and drained
- 1/2 cup cooked quinoa

- 1/2 cup diced carrots
- 1/2 cup diced cucumber
- 1/4 cup chopped fresh parsley
- 2 tablespoons olive oil
- 1 tablespoon apple cider vinegar
- 1 teaspoon honey

Step by Step Preparations

- In a large mixing bowl, combine the diced chicken breast, cooked chickpeas, cooked quinoa, diced carrots, diced cucumber, and chopped fresh parsley.
- In a small bowl, whisk together the olive oil, apple cider vinegar, and honey to make the dressing.
- Pour the dressing over the chicken and chickpea mixture and toss until well combined.
- Serve immediately or refrigerate for later use.

Nutritional Information (per serving):

Calories: 150 calories, Protein: 15g, Fat: 6g, Carbohydrates: 10g, Fiber: 2g

40. Turkey and Oatmeal Bake

Serving Size: ½ cup

Yield: 4

Ingredients

- 1 lb lean ground turkey
- 1 cup cooked oatmeal, plain unsweetened
- 1/2 cup cooked mixed vegetables like carrots, green beans, peas.
- 1/4 cup plain Greek yogurt
- 1 tablespoon olive oil

Step by Step Preparations

•Preheat your oven to 350°F (175°C). Grease a baking dish with olive oil and set aside.

•In a large mixing bowl, combine the lean ground turkey, cooked oatmeal, and cooked mixed vegetables. Mix well until all ingredients are evenly distributed.

•Transfer the mixture into the greased baking dish and spread it out evenly.

•Bake in the preheated oven for 25-30 minutes or until the turkey is cooked through and lightly browned on top.

•Remove from the oven and let it cool slightly before serving.

•Top each serving with a dollop of plain Greek yogurt for added flavor and moisture.

Nutritional Information (per serving):

Calories: 150 kcal, Protein: 15g, Fat: 6g, Carbohydrates: 8g, Fiber: 1 gram

Homemade Dog Treats for Small Dogs

41. Peanut Butter Banana Bites

Serving Size: 1-2 per day

Yield: 20-24

Ingredients

- 1 ripe banana, mashed
- 1/4 cup natural peanut butter unsalted (no added sugar)
- 1 cup oats, old-fashioned or quick-cooking.

•1 tablespoon honey (avoid if your dog has diabetes or is overweight)

Step by Step Preparations

•Preheat your oven to 350°F (175°C) and line a baking sheet with parchment paper.

•In a mixing bowl, combine the mashed banana, peanut butter, oats, and honey (if using). Mix until well combined and form a thick dough.

•Roll the dough into small bite-sized balls, 1 teaspoon each, and place them on the prepared baking sheet.

•Use a fork to gently flatten each ball into a small disc shape.

•Bake in the preheated oven for 10-12 minutes or until the treats are golden brown and firm to the touch.

•Remove from the oven and allow the treats to cool completely on the baking sheet.

•Once cooled, transfer the treats to an airtight container and store them in the refrigerator for up to one week or freeze for longer storage.

Nutritional Information (per treat):

Calories: 30-40 calorie, Protein: 1-2 g, Fat: 1-2 g, Carbohydrates: 3-4 g,Fiber: 0.5-1 gram

---

42. Sweet Potato Chews

Serving Size: 1 slice

Yield: 20–30

Ingredients

•2 medium sweet potatoes

Step by Step Preparations

•Preheat your oven to 250°F (120°C) and line a baking sheet with parchment paper.

•Wash the sweet potatoes thoroughly and pat them dry with a clean towel.

•Cut the sweet potatoes into thin slices about 1/4 inch thick. You can also cut them into strips or rounds depending on your preference.

•Arrange the sweet potato slices in a single layer on the prepared baking sheet, make sure they are not overlapping.

•Bake the sweet potato slices in the preheated oven for 2-3 hours or until they are dry and crispy. Flip them halfway through the baking time to ensure even cooking.

•Once the sweet potato slices are crispy and fully dried, remove them from the oven and allow them to cool completely.

- Store in an airtight container at room temperature for up to two weeks, or in the refrigerator for longer shelf life.

Nutritional Information (per serving):

Calories: 30, Protein: 0.5g, Fat: 0g, Carbohydrates: 7g, Fiber: 1g

---

43. Carrot and Oat Biscuits

Serving Size: 1

Yield: 12

Ingredients

- 1 cup rolled oats
- 1/2 cup shredded carrots
- 1/4 cup unsweetened applesauce
- 1 tablespoon coconut oil (melted)

• 1 egg

Step by Step Preparations

• Preheat your oven to 350°F (175°C). Line a baking sheet with parchment paper.

• In a large mixing bowl, combine the rolled oats, shredded carrots, applesauce, melted coconut oil, and egg. Stir until well combined and the mixture forms a dough-like consistency.

• Roll out the dough on a lightly floured surface to about 1/4 inch thickness.

• Use a cookie cutter to cut out biscuit shapes from the dough. Place the biscuits on the prepared baking sheet.

• Bake in the preheated oven for 15-20 minutes, or until the biscuits are golden brown and firm to the touch.

- Remove from the oven and let cool completely on a wire rack.

- Once cooled, store in an airtight container at room temperature or in the refrigerator for up to one week.

Nutritional Information (per biscuit):

Calories: 50, Protein: 1.5 g, Fat: 2 g, Carbohydrates: 7 g, Fiber: 1 gram, Calcium: 6.5 mg, Iron: 0.5 mg

---

44. Chicken and Cheese Bites

Serving Size: 1

Yield: 24

Ingredients

- 1 cup cooked chicken shredded
- 1/2 cup grated cheese (such as cheddar or mozzarella)

- 1 egg
- 1 cup oat flour (you can make your own by grinding rolled oats in a blender or food processor until fine)

Step by Step Preparations

- Preheat your oven to 350°F (180°C) and line a baking sheet with parchment paper.
- In a large mixing bowl combine the cooked chicken, grated cheese, egg, and oat flour. Mix well until all ingredients are evenly combined.
- Roll the dough into small balls about 1 inch in diameter, and place them on the prepared baking sheet.
- Use a fork to flatten each ball slightly until a disc like shape is created

- Bake in the preheated oven for 15-20 minutes or until the treats are golden brown and firm to the touch.

- Remove from the oven and allow the treats to cool completely on a wire rack.

- Once cooled, store in an airtight container in the refrigerator for up to one week.

Nutritional Information (per serving):

Calories: 35, Protein: 3g, Fat: 2g, Carbohydrates: 1g, Fiber: 0.5g, Calcium: 20mg, Iron: 0.5mg, Potassium: 25mg

---

45. Blueberry and Oat Bars

Serving Size: 1

Yield: 12

Ingredients

- 1 cup rolled oats

- 1/2 cup blueberries, fresh or frozen.

- 1 ripe banana mashed

- 1/4 cup unsweetened applesauce

- 1 tablespoon honey (optional)

Step by Step Preparations

- Preheat your oven to 350°F (175°C). Line a baking sheet with parchment paper or lightly grease it with cooking spray.

- In a mixing bowl, combine the rolled oats, mashed banana, unsweetened applesauce, and honey (if using). Mix well until all ingredients are thoroughly combined.

- Gently fold in the blueberries, be careful not to crush them too much.

- Spread the mixture evenly onto the prepared baking sheet, smooth it out with a spatula.

- Bake in the preheated oven for 20-25 minutes or until the edges are golden brown and the bars are firm to the touch.
- Remove from the oven and let cool completely before cutting into bars or squares.

Nutritional Information (per serving):

Calories: 45 kcal, Protein: 1.1 g, Fat: 0.5 g, Carbohydrates: 9.5 g, Fiber: 1.2 g, Sugars: 3.7 g

46. Pumpkin and Cinnamon Cookies

Serving Size: 1

Yield: 24–30

Ingredients

- 1 cup canned pumpkin puree (not pumpkin pie filling)
- 2 cups whole wheat flour (or oat flour for gluten-free option)

- 1 teaspoon ground cinnamon
- 1 egg
- Splash of water

Step by Step Preparations

- Preheat your oven to 350°F (175°C) and line a baking sheet with parchment paper.
- In a large mixing bowl, combine the pumpkin puree, whole wheat flour, ground cinnamon, and egg. Mix until well combined. If the dough is too dry, add a splash of water to achieve a workable consistency.
- Roll out the dough on a lightly floured surface to about 1/4 inch thickness.
- Use cookie cutters to cut out shapes or simply use a knife to cut the dough into small squares or rectangles.

• Place the cut-out dough onto the prepared baking sheet, leave a little space between each cookie.

• Bake in the preheated oven for 15-20 minutes or until the cookies are firm and golden brown.

• Allow the cookies to cool completely on a wire rack before serving.

Nutritional Information (per serving):

Calories: 30 calories per cookie, Protein: 1.5g,Fat: 0.5g, Carbohydrates: 6g, Fiber: 1 gram, Calcium: 5mg, Iron: 0.5 mg

---

47. Tuna and Parsley Balls

Serving Size: 1

Yield: 12

Ingredients

- 1 can of tuna in water drained
- 1/2 cup rolled oats
- 1/4 cup chopped fresh parsley
- 1 egg
- 1 tablespoon olive oil

Step by Step Preparations

- Preheat your oven to 350°F (175°C). Line a baking sheet with parchment paper.
- In a food processor or blender, combine the drained tuna, rolled oats, chopped parsley, egg, and olive oil. Blend until the mixture forms a thick uniform dough.
- Scoop out tablespoon-sized portions of the dough and roll them into balls using your

hands. Place the balls on the prepared baking sheet.

•Bake the tuna and parsley balls in the preheated oven for 15-20 minutes or until firm and lightly golden brown.

•Remove the treats from the oven and allow them to cool completely before serving.

Nutritional Information (per serving):

Calories: 35 kcal, Protein: 3g, Fat: 2g, Carbohydrates: 1g, Fiber: 0.5g, Calcium: 6mg, Iron: 0.4mg, Potassium: 37 mg

---

48. Apple and Cinnamon Biscuits

Serving Size: ¼ biscuit

Yield: 24 small biscuits

Ingredients

- 1 cup finely chopped apple peeled and cored

- 1 1/2 cups whole wheat flour

- 1/4 cup oatmeal

- 1/2 teaspoon ground cinnamon

- 1 egg

- 1/4 cup water or unsweetened applesauce

Step by Step Preparations

- Preheat your oven to 350°F (175°C). Line a baking sheet with parchment paper or lightly grease it.

- In a mixing bowl, combine the finely chopped apple, whole wheat flour, oatmeal, and ground cinnamon.

- In a separate small bowl, beat the egg, then add it to the dry ingredients along with the water or applesauce. Mix until a dough forms.

Add a little more water if necessary to achieve the right consistency.

•Roll out the dough on a floured surface to about 1/4-inch thickness. Use cookie cutters to cut out biscuit shapes.

•Place the biscuits on the prepared baking sheet and bake for 20-25 minutes or until golden brown and firm to the touch.

•Allow the biscuits to cool completely before serving. Store any leftovers in an airtight container in the refrigerator for up to one week.

Nutritional Information

Calories per Serving: 8 kcal, Protein: 0.3g, Fat: 0.1g, Carbohydrates: 1.4g, Fiber: 0.2g

---

49. Spinach and Cheese Squares

Serving Size: 1

Ingredients

- 1 cup cooked spinach chopped
- 1 cup shredded low-fat cheese such as cheddar or mozzarella
- 1 cup oat flour or whole wheat flour
- 1 egg
- 1 tablespoon olive oil

Step by Step Preparations

- Preheat your oven to 350°F (175°C) and line a baking sheet with parchment paper.
- In a large mixing bowl, combine the cooked spinach, shredded cheese, oat flour, egg, and olive oil. Mix well until all ingredients are evenly combined.

•Press the mixture into the prepared baking sheet, spread it out evenly to form a square or rectangle shape.

•Bake in the preheated oven for 20-25 minutes or until the edges are golden brown and the mixture is set.

•Remove from the oven and allow to cool completely before cutting into squares or bite-sized pieces.

•Store the spinach and cheese squares in an airtight container in the refrigerator for up to one week, or freeze for longer storage.

Nutritional Information (per serving):

Calories: 40, Protein: 2g, Fat: 2g, Carbohydrates: 4g, Fiber: 1g, Calcium: 35mg, Iron: 0.5mg

---

50. Cranberry and Turkey Meatballs

Serving Size: 1

Yield: 20

Ingredients

- 1 lb lean ground turkey
- 1/2 cup dried cranberries (unsweetened)
- 1/4 cup rolled oats uncooked
- 1 egg
- 1 tablespoon olive oil
- 1 teaspoon dried parsley

Step by Step Preparations

- Preheat your oven to 350°F (175°C) and line a baking sheet with parchment paper or a silicone baking mat.
- In a large mixing bowl, combine the ground turkey, dried cranberries, rolled oats, egg, olive oil, and dried parsley. Mix until well combined.

- Roll the mixture into small meatballs, about the size of a tablespoon, and place them evenly spaced on the prepared baking sheet.
- Bake the meatballs in the preheated oven for 15-20 minutes or until cooked through and lightly browned on the outside.
- Remove the meatballs from the oven and allow them to cool completely before serving to your dog.

Nutritional Information (per meatball):

Calories: 30 kcal, Protein: 3g, Fat:1g, Carbohydrates: 2g, Fiber: 0.5g, Sugars: 1 g, Calcium: 5 mg, Iron: 0.3 mg, Sodium: 10 mg

---

EXPERT ADVICE

Any leftovers can be frozen for longer storage (thaw frozen portions in the refrigerator overnight before serving) or portion them into individual servings and store in an airtight container in the refrigerator for up to three days.

Conversion Charts

Dry Ingredients

USA (Cups)	UK (Metric)
1 cup	240 ml
½ cup	120 ml
⅓ cup	80 ml
¼ cup	60 ml
1 tablespoon	15 ml
1 teaspoon	5 ml

Liquid Ingredients

USA (Fluid Ounces)	UK (Metric)
1 fluid ounce	30 ml

½ fluid ounce	15 ml
¼ fluid ounce	7.5 ml
⅛ ounce	3.75 ml
1 tablespoon	15 ml
1 teaspoon	5 ml

GO AND COOK THOSE DELICIOUS HEALTHY MEALS FOR YOUR DOG.

END.

www.ingramcontent.com/pod-product-compliance
Lightning Source LLC
LaVergne TN
LVHW022016230425
809438LV00008B/161